# Blagging it

*Reflections of a rookie Seasonaire*

*For my Espace Killy family:*

*Cathers, Foz, Jo, John, Matt, Winks and Woodsy.*

*In gratitude and affection.*

Kindle Direct Publishing
Copyright © 2024 Tom Cowie
All rights reserved.

# Blag
## (Verb – UK Informal)

*'To persuade someone in a clever or slightly dishonest way to allow you to do something'.*

**Cambridge Dictionary**

# L'introduction

Deciding to take the plunge and work a ski season in France remains one of the biggest gambles I have ever taken, and the memories and lasting friendships that endure to this day are proof of 'Del Boy' Trotter's sage wisdom that (sometimes at least), *'he who dares, wins'*.

I've always been a fairly risk-averse character. I rarely gamble, snubbing the potential windfall in favour of the actual money residing in my wallet. When I do have a flutter, it will be on a sporting event where I will feel that my knowledge of the protagonists involved gives me a half decent chance of seeing a return. This approach wouldn't have applied to ski seasons, or even skiing, with my firsthand experience prior to going to Tignes consisting of a week in Méribel with an old university friend a few years earlier.

In this context, the decision that I took is even more remarkable, and the outcome even more satisfying. It's probably why my memories of those days in Tignes Eighteen years ago remain so vivid, and the reason that I have been able to commit so many of them to the page with relative ease. Like pulling a dusty box of belongings off the top of a cupboard only to find another one concealed behind it, the process of writing has unearthed further recollections, all of which have helped to transport me back in time every time I have sat in front of my laptop and started typing.

There is a time and a place for making spontaneous, slightly self-indulgent decisions which becomes harder with each passing year, as adult life and the responsibilities that come with it take on greater and greater significance. It's for that reason, that if one day, one of my children asks me whether I think they should do a ski season, I know what my response will be – an unequivocal yes. Whether they do one season or many, they will experience places, people, and situations unique to that environment, creating memories which will last a lifetime.

Here are a few of mine……

# 1

# Un petit mensonge blanc

I can't really recall the moment that I decided that I was going to down tools in London and embark on a ski season. It was an itch I had been meaning to scratch since hearing about my two older sister's respective seasons in years gone by, but after three post graduate years working in the capital, the itch seemed destined to remain just that. I was twenty-five, and earning decent money, which was divided each month between the rent on my Putney flat, and the various bars of SW15.
Then fate intervened.
In a decision which I look back on as being brave and reckless in equal measure, (ah the impetuosity of youth), I had resigned from my job at an ad agency for no reason other than the fact that I was bored of it. It was September, and with the 2006/7 ski season just around the corner, I decided that this would be my best, and possibly last chance to scratch the aforementioned itch. When I discovered that Skiworld's headquarters were just down the road in Hammersmith, I decided it was written in the stars.
The larger tour operators such as Thompson had fairly robust online application processes that would have probably found me wanting on a few box ticking fronts. Skiworld on the other hand were proud of the fact that they were the UK's largest independent tour operator and seemed to pervade a more personal, old-school approach which appealed to me, and my *modus operandi*.

So, having filled in the fairly basic questionnaire, I duly received an invitation to attend an interview. I set out from Putney with little idea of the journey that I was about to embark on, or the people that I would be destined to meet along the way. Being the right sort of age for a resort rep, I played to my strengths in the interview. *Did I have management experience?* Tick. *Could I speak French competently enough to get by?* Tick. *Could I drive?* Tick. *Could I manage emotional and potential tricky customer situations?* Tick.

As I turned to leave the room, the lady interviewing me said, almost in passing 'oh and I assume you can ski?'.

It was a perfectly reasonable question, rather like asking someone taking part in a track day if they had a driving license.

'Of course,' I said confidently, adding, (with a hint of modesty) 'but I'm a bit rusty'.

'I'm sure you'll be fine' she replied, 'but we have to ask as we offer free ski guiding for our guests which is part of the rep's job'.

A few weeks later, I had confirmation of my post interview optimism – I would be departing for Tignes in November to become a resort rep for the 2006/7 ski season.

En route to Tignes there would be a training week in Courchevel, ironically, the location of both of my sister's ski seasons. As the departure date approached, the magnitude of what I was about to do began to set in. I wondered how I would cope guiding guests on the mountain with the sum total of one week's skiing experience under my belt, cunningly disguised in the interview as good old fashioned English modesty.

However, I reassured myself that I would have plenty of time to quietly reacquaint myself with a pair of skis before the business of the season started, and no one would be any the wiser for the little white lie I had told back in Hammersmith.

# 2

# Le voyage commence

Before we left British soil, there was a large fancy dress party in London for all resort bound UK staff. The next day, the contingent of reps would attend a cooking course to ensure that in the event of the chalet staff being incapacitated by the dreaded gastroenteritis, we would be able to rustle up a three-course dinner for our guests in their absence.

I've never been a fan of fancy dress, but decided it was important to make some effort. Still, I felt like a prize lemon walking down Putney High Street dressed as Maverick from *Top Gun*, complete with 'flight suit' and aviator sunglasses. The party was fairly forgettable – unlike the hangover which stalked me relentlessly the next day on the cookery course.

Through the alcohol induced brain fog, I did manage to remember our cookery instructor's golden rule. Namely, that almost all savoury dishes worth cooking start with the humble onion. I might not have been able to ski, but I could at least now rustle up a tomato and mozzarella stack, pork Lyonnaise, and chocolate torte.

I remember posting my keys through the letterbox of my flat and hauling my bags the short distance up the high street to the train station. Contained within them was my Skiworld uniform, which we had been 'fitted' for in Hammersmith in a scene reminiscent of the ones in films when new prison inmates move along a line to receive their standard issue fatigues. My navy polo shirts and fetching grey chords would see plenty of use over the next six months, but none afterwards.

We were flown out to resort but warned that we couldn't expect such lavish treatment on the way back. That was all too far away to worry about though, and as I jetted off from Gatwick bound for Geneva, I remember still not being quite able to comprehend what I was doing, what I had given up, or why.

# 3

# Courchevel et la naissance de 'Bambi'

Will picked us up at the airport. A Somerset boy, he was slightly younger than me but was a seasoned campaigner of numerous winter and summer seasons, and more than knew his way round a resort, not to mention a piste, often electing to ski 'switch', (which I later learned meant backwards.) The arrivals terminal was where I also met the rest of the team who would make the next six months so memorable.

Catherine (or Cathers as she quickly became known) was a no-nonsense Yorkshire lass who had done a season or two previously, and who would pride herself on being the mother hen of our team. It had been during the previous season that she had met Jess (quickly nicknamed Foz on account of her surname). Hailing from Bristol, Foz wore big, hooped earrings, smoked 'rollies', and had one of the dirtiest cackles I had ever heard.

John and Matt were twins from Northern Ireland. John would be the fifth member of our Tignes rep's group, whilst Matt would be based across the valley in Val D'Isère with Jo, who like Will, was no stranger to resort life. Together, it would be our job to rep the 300km Espace Killy ski region for Skiworld. After a near death experience on the way courtesy of Will's questionable interpretation of French motorway laws, we arrived in Courchevel to begin our training week.

Amongst a host of fairly dull classes, the week was memorable for two things. Firstly, it's where I watched the '06 – '07 Ashes series get off to a false start, as a group of us crowded around the TV in the hotel bar at 1am to witness Steve Harmison infamously bowl the first delivery of the match to his mate Andrew Flintoff who was standing at second slip. It was also when I received the nickname that has stayed firmly attached to me by my Skiworld colleagues to this day.

Whilst not yet experiencing much snow, the resort was certainly very icy. It's fair to say that loafers were probably not the most appropriate footwear, although one could argue that they were the ideal choice of footwear for someone blagging their way on to a ski season. Unfortunately, the shoes welched on the deal rather sooner than anticipated.

One afternoon, I had the most enormous fall (or 'stack' to use the skiing vernacular that I was rapidly learning), ending up with my feet pointing skyward, before crashing down to earth on the small of my back. As I scrabbled around to find traction between my leather soles and the sheet ice beneath them, Matt commented that I looked like 'Bambi on ice'. And with that, my alter ego was born.

# 4

# Bienvenue à Tignes!

When we finally arrived in Tignes, I was able to meet the remaining members of our management team. Cat, the resort accountant, and the resort manager, Chris, or 'Woodsy' as he was universally known.

Woodsy had plenty of seasons under his belt and knew Tignes like the back of his hand. He knew how the place ran, everyone else who worked in it, and how to get the best out of it. His experience was invaluable, and we quickly gelled into a close-knit team. We also met all the chalet staff who had been on a different training week, and who to a man, immediately started calling me Bambi as well (apparently it wasn't just gastroenteritis that could quickly spread throughout a resort.)

One tradition that Woodsy wanted to maintain was that in the days prior to the first guests arriving, we would all ski together as a total resort staff, the only time this would happen. A combination of panic and nausea now spread over me, with the realisation that my plan to quietly reacquaint myself with the slopes had been scuppered. My deception in the interview was about to be very publicly exposed.

My fate was sealed when, gingerly emerging from the top of the funicular, I mistook a black marker for a blue one. What my new colleagues must have thought as they were overtaken by a human snowball is anyone's guess. Cathers took pity on me and stopped to help me retrieve my kit. As she did so, and with a slightly incredulous look on her face, she asked me if I knew that we would be guiding three days a week for the next six months? At that point, I'd have struggled to get down a nursery slope, never mind guide someone else down one.

I had surprisingly few 'wipe outs' after this, probably because I was a conservative skier who kept recreational piste visits to a minimum, but one of the occasions when I did have a fall was memorable for a comment made by a total stranger.

Whilst making my merry (and no doubt pedestrian) way down a slope, I caught an edge and hit the deck before I could even register what had happened. Various pieces of equipment liberated themselves from my body as I tumbled down the hill, and as I got to my feet, I turned back up the piste to see a snowboarder, slaloming through the debris field I had created.

'Nice yard sale' yelled an American voice as he flew by. Despite having an ice burnt face and a mouthful of snow, I had to laugh.

So, my secret was out, and I was unceremoniously banned from guiding until deemed to be of a good enough standard. Skiworld generously paid for me to have lessons for six weeks, by which point I was adjudged to be proficient enough to get myself (and our guests) down the hill in one piece.

Speaking of arriving in one piece reminds me of my first memory of Woodsy. On arrival in Tignes, I discovered that I would be based in *Val Claret* at the top of the resort. A lake separates *Val Claret* from the centre of the resort, *Le Lac*, with the third part of the resort, *Le Lavachet*, beyond that. All three areas were linked by a free shuttle bus service.

Seasonnaire life is punctuated by colourful characters like Woodsy, who possess a sense of *joie de vivre* – occasionally reckless, seldom dangerous, never malicious, but always supportive. This is critical given the role of a resort manager is to mould a group of strangers into a team capable of working in each other's pockets 24/7, performing repetitive tasks in a claustrophobic, and sometimes pressurised environment, week in, week out.

Woodsy had offered to drive me up to my apartment, and as we approached a mini roundabout in Val Claret, he spotted an opportunity to give a rookie seasonaire a baptism in resort culture. One trip round the roundabout was swiftly followed by a second, then even more quickly, a third. At this point the laws of physics overpowered the rear of the car, and it broke free. We were now drifting round the roundabout with the tyres of the Peugeot screeching, as Woodsy threw back his Oakley adorned head, laughing maniacally in the manner that would become so familiar.

Once we had stopped circulating around the local traffic calming measures, he dropped me off at my apartment. It was usually allocated to the resort manager, but Woodsy had his own flat, so whilst my colleagues were sharing modest lodgings down in *Le Lac*, my home for the next six months would consist of a spacious apartment which included double bed and balcony, all to myself.

# 5

# Premiers jours

Located at 2,100 metres above sea level, Tignes boasts one of the longest winter seasons in Europe. The guests started arriving in late November, and they would keep coming until mid-May. However, it's fair to say that after my first week on official duty, I was questioning whether I would still be around by then. I was responsible for forty-eight guests each week, spread across four properties; *Tichot,* a standalone chalet*,* and *Valerie, Dominique* and *Francois*, which were one on top of the other, with a communal spa in the basement.

In the first week of the season, *Dominique* and *Francois* were booked by Exeter University ski club, and fuelled by alcohol and reckless indifference, half of my first intake of guests ran amok. The weekly allocation of wine disappeared on the first night, (not for the last time that season), and I was woken the next morning by a call from our resort maintenance man Adam (or 'Bee Gee' as he had been renamed) asking me if I had seen the front of one of my properties.

With a deep sense of trepidation, I walked the short distance from my apartment to the chalet, where I discovered that all the empty wine bottles had been launched off the balcony by the drunken undergraduates, resulting in the entire area in front of the chalet being covered with shards of glass, poking menacingly out of the snow like a shiver of sharks during a feeding frenzy.

The incident, and its ramifications, which involved me reading the riot act to the hungover group before dinner that night, marked the end of my honeymoon period, and an insight into the realities of what I had signed up for. Whilst I hadn't considered beforehand the potential perils of riotous students descending on my little patch of the resort, the thought of a guest injuring themselves and how I would act in those circumstances certainly had crossed my mind during our training week.

I didn't have long to wait before I had acquired firsthand experience of the situation, when a couple of weeks later, one of my guests fell on the slopes and ruptured her cruciate ligament. Frustratingly for her, the injury occurred on her first day, condemning her to a week of reading books and filling out insurance paperwork (with limited help from her rep), whilst her friends continued to enjoy themselves on the hill.

Within a few weeks I was fully settled into the weekly routine which governed our lives and ensured that everything ran as smoothly and consistently as possible from one week to the next. One weekly occurrence which never got any easier however, was Saturday - the infamous 'changeover' day.

# 6

# Samedi

Prior to embarking on a ski season, Saturdays had always consisted of using free time as I pleased. Now they took on the guise of Mondays, ushering in the new working week with an eighteen - hour marathon. Whilst the day's routine became more and more familiar, it never got any easier, and every Saturday evening was met with the same feeling of exhaustion and relief.

My alarm would go off at 3.30am, and having showered and changed into my uniform, I would walk down to Le Lac, where three or four coaches would be waiting for us, their drivers often huddled together, clutching thermos mugs of coffee and quietly chatting beneath a haze of Gauloises smoke.

I can vividly remember the attack on the senses during those walks; emerging into the cold, crisp air with the taste of toothpaste in my mouth, and my hair still damp from the shower. There was a nightclub near my apartment block, and I would pass amongst late night revellers, for whom the previous day had not yet ended. From there I would cross the frozen lake, which separated two parts of the resort.

There were no people around now - just an eerie silence, broken only by the noise of the snow crunching beneath my feet. The stars shone bright and clear overhead from a jet-black sky. High above, and surrounding me on all sides, the perpetual darkness of the mountain was interspersed by tiny moving lights, like an army of illuminated ants, as the piste combing machines continued their lonely work preparing the slopes for the day ahead.

Upon boarding your designated bus, the first task was to assess the driver. With the odd exception, they reinforced the negative English stereotype of a French truck driver. Sullen and morose, they were masterful exponents of the shoulder shrug, which was often deployed as a preferable alternative to demonstrating any English language skills that they possessed.

It was always worth plotting the optimum route round the resort in advance, as trying to think on your feet in French with an uncooperative driver, on snow covered mountain roads at 4am was a sure way of getting a long day off to a bad start. Having heard horror stories of children's vomit running down the aisle as the bus wound its way down the mountain, I was always relieved if my pickup list proved to be *sans enfant*.

For the other reps, it was a trip to Chambery, Lyon or Geneva airport, which would afford a chance of some additional sleep, but with the exception of a few early season forays to Lyon airport, I never went further than Moutiers, a transport hub about an hour's drive from resort.

I had the dubious honour of repping the Eurostar, better known locally as the *Ski Train*. Essentially a mobile night club, it travelled overnight from London, allowing its occupants to be skiing by Saturday lunchtime, thereby giving them an extra half day on the mountain compared to their airborne peers.

At Moutiers I would meet Skiworld staff who, during the week, were based at the main office in Bourg St. Maurice. They would spend most of their Saturday at Moutiers, coordinating the numerous coaches carrying hundreds of guests on their way to and from various resorts. Some of them I only ever saw there – at 6am, slightly dishevelled, wrapped in multiple layers, armed with a coffee, quietly contemplating the next 12 hours, and hoping it would pass without too much incident.

Boarding the 'ski train' at Moutiers, I would start knocking on compartment doors, and 'repping.' This consisted of the selling of lift passes, ski hire equipment and lessons for the week, and would be what my colleagues would be doing on their respective coaches returning from the airports. I had about 30 minutes from boarding at Moutiers to the train arriving in Bourg St. Maurice. From there, I would have around 40 minutes to complete the task as the bus wound its way up the mountain to resort, where a firm footing and an even firmer constitution was essential.

Having dropped the guests off at their properties, I would go to the lift pass office, having first relieved each of them of their passport, as these were required in order for a lift pass to be issued. Returning with the passports and about £2,000 of lift passes, I would then book in lessons with ESF (the official French ski school) and drop the equipment orders into the ski hire company, who would quickly dispatch Land Rovers filled with kit to the relevant properties.

On entering a chalet with my valuable quarry, I would always encounter the same scene; bags being unpacked, pastries and coffee being hurriedly consumed, piste maps being pored over, and missing gloves and socks being searched for. Guests would wander around in various stages of undress, with at least one of their number engaged in a furious battle with the fastening of their salopettes, as the excesses of the previous 12 months since they were last worn became apparent.

By now it would be about 11am, and time to go and do my sales accounts with Cat, our resort accountant. This was always preceded by a cooked breakfast that Cat made for me and Woodsy in her apartment, which provided a welcome break after such a long morning.

In addition to catered chalets, Skiworld also had some self-catering properties in the resort, so by 1pm, I would be getting the keys from the letting agent in *Le Lac* and showing the guests into their apartments as they arrived. By 3 or 4pm depending on which airport they had been to, the others would all be back in resort, and the five of us would once again converge on Cat's flat, so that they could go through their sales accounts with her.

This process was agonising, especially for me, who had done my accounts hours earlier, but we always stayed together – there was no sloping off early. It was a golden rule, along with the company wide rule that skiing was forbidden on transfer day. I'd get home about 9pm, usually picking up a pizza on the way. But there would be no Sunday lie in.

# 7

# Dimanche

Sunday mornings in many ways were harder than Saturdays – with the latter you didn't have a chance to feel tired, but on Sunday, you were wiped out from the day before. First up was a trip to the ESF office to collect the guest's lesson vouchers that I had booked in the previous day.

There were always a few ESF instructors loitering around and flirting with the office staff. Never seen without their sunglasses, these bronzed alpha males strutted through the resort like peacocks, resplendent in their bright red ESF uniforms. Their English language skills and patience levels when instructing on the mountain were often influenced by the gender of the student, or their skiing ability. One week, the ramifications of this attitude landed unceremoniously on my doorstep.

One evening, whilst conducting my daily rounds, I was approached by one of the guests, who explained that his girlfriend, who had no skiing experience, had booked into ski school each morning, allowing him, a more experienced skier, to explore the mountain before they were reunited at lunchtime. On the first day, she had been walked off the mountain by the exasperated instructor, leaving her in tears, and her boyfriend now unable to ski with his friends in the mornings.

This was a classic example of an issue which would be blamed on the rep (I sold the lessons after all), even though we had no control over which instructor was allocated to each group. Unusually, there was a young Scotsman working for ESF that season, who I got chatting to one day. I explained the issues we were having with some of his French colleagues, and he agreed to help me where he could.

From that point on, I was occasionally able to book my guests in with the one British ESF instructor in Tignes, which provided me with extra brownie points on my weekly customer survey score, whilst ensuring an incident free week of lessons - for some of the guests at least.

Having collected the lesson vouchers, it was then on to the chalets to deliver them to the guests over breakfast. This was my first 'official' chalet trip of the week, and it would inevitably involve answering all the typical first day questions; *'Can I swap my ski boots?' 'Where's a good place for lunch on the mountain?'*, and by far the most common, *'What's the snow going to be like this week?'*.

e maps would be thrust at me, accompanied by pointing fingers and enquiring eyes. When asked to comment on the difficulty of various black runs, I would answer in an assured, yet politely modest tone. The implication was that I could ski any of them backwards on one leg, when in fact, I hadn't attempted any of them following my embarrassing, accidental foray down one on my first outing.

For those who wanted to quickly familiarise themselves with the mountain, there would be a half day guide available in the morning. We offered two half days, and one full day guide each week. These were offered by the company free of charge, as a 'value add'.

In hindsight, this was probably just as well, as the 'value' you derived from your excursion bore a direct correlation to the competence of the guide leading you. Sufficed to say, I tended to be the 'rear gunner', ensuring that no stragglers were left behind, but not having to think about where we were actually going, which was left to Will, who tended to be my guiding partner.

On one of the rare occasions that I led the group, I was without a rear gunner. It was just me, and a group of expectant tourists. Leading the group down a piste, I was confronted by a chair lift on my left, and another further down the slope in the distance. Which one to choose? I picked the wrong one, leading the group back to the top of the run that we had just come down.

Often, I was the greater beneficiary of these solo expeditions, discovering runs that I had hitherto not experienced, courtesy of one of the slightly exasperated guests who had taken over as the expedition leader.

On Sunday evening, the five of us plus Cat and Woodsy always went out for dinner. I loved those nights – we'd trade stories of difficult French bus drivers, delayed flights, and impatient, intoxicated, or vomiting guests over numerous bottles of wine. Despite being tired, there was always a sense of optimism in the air that we had ticked off another weekend, and now it was plain sailing until the next one came around.

# 8

# Lundi, Mardi, et Jeudi

The midweek routine consisted of a combination of chalet visits in the morning and evening (it's fair to say my evening attendance record was better than my morning one), ski guiding, driving the chalet staff to the supermarket in Bourg St. Maurice, and running apres ski events in the evening, which is where we made our money.

All these tasks and activities were managed on a rota system, to try and ensure some variation in an otherwise formulaic and repetitive week. The chalet visits on Sunday evening often made or broke our week, for it was here that you pitched the various après ski activities and tried to sign up as many people as possible to the bar crawl, quiz night, and our star attraction, ice karting.

A local family had built a floodlit ice track in Val Claret with karts that ran on spiked tyres. From an insurance point of view, it was dubious at best had anything gone wrong, but fortunately it never did. I did have one near miss, when, whilst acting as a trackside marshal, I had to dive over the barrier to avoid being wiped out by a kart which was spinning out of control.

Thanks to ice karting, we were often each pocketing well over E100 a week, which was more than enough, considering our living and skiing costs were covered by the company. On more than one occasion I reinvested some of my weekly wages in additional trips to the track which was opposite my apartment. It proved to be an opportunity unique to that season, as it was deemed too risky by the incoming resort manager the following year.

I was at least able to back up one of my claims made during my interview – that I was competent when it came to speaking the local dialect. This resulted in me being made responsible for managing our considerable weekly bread order, as neither the local baker nor his wife spoke a word of English.

Every Thursday I was dispatched from Cat's apartment with a fat envelope full of cash which I swiftly delivered to the baker, along with any revisions to our weekly order, which ran to hundreds of baguettes. Without fail, my arrival (and that of the fat envelope) was greeted with hushed revery.

No matter how busy the shop was, I was always ushered to a table where espresso and pastries would appear before me. What would then follow would be a slightly one - sided conversation, interjected by occasional comments and gestures from me, as my schoolboy French vocab was stretched to its limit.

# 9

# Mercredi

Wednesday was our day off, and was almost always accompanied by a hangover, following our escapades the night before. We'd often drive over to Val D'Isère and spend it with Matt and Jo in places like *Saloon Bar*, and the infamous *Dick's Tea Bar*. The scale of some of the hangovers we used to suffer is easier to understand when one considers the drinks which proceeded them.

Standard issue in *Saloon* was a pint of Long Island iced tea. Whilst I knew we were all making good money, I used to be quietly surprised that everyone was happy to pay so much for a round of these potent cocktails. It wasn't until about two months into the season that I realised that the reason for this was *Saloon's* Seasonaire discount which I, (and my wallet) had hitherto been unaware of. Needless to say, my request to have two months of the equivalent discount value on credit was swiftly refused.

In *Dicks Tea Bar* we would often end up in the VIP area with a bottle of vodka or gin courtesy of the manager who was a friend of Matt and John's from Northern Ireland. Sometimes Jo and Matt would come over to Tignes instead, where the evening would inevitably finish in *Jack's* nightclub in Le Lac, where more free drinks would come our way via its owner, the redoubtable *Martine*.

A no-nonsense publican, she clearly believed in actions speaking louder than words. A nod or hand gesture directed towards one of her members of staff could result in the serving of a drink on the house - or being escorted off the premises. Fortunately, in our case, it was often the former, but I did witness a few well lubricated tourists falling foul of the latter.

Whilst most spent their day off skiing, I found a different way of clearing the cobwebs, in the more gentile surroundings of *Fish Tank* or *Jam Bar*, where I'd enjoy breakfast, a coffee, and a read of the paper. My reputation as someone who was more in love with resort lifestyle rather than the skiing itself was one well earned.

Guests fended for themselves on a Wednesday night, and we would book them in to local restaurants for a set menu dinner, which would include a variety of traditional alpine dishes such as raclette and fondu. It worked well for everyone – the guests got a good value three course dinner, the restaurants were guaranteed to be full, and consequently, we rarely had to put our hands in our pockets when we went there ourselves.

I was desperate to put a marker down and show my credentials, which clearly wasn't going to happen on the piste, so I resolved that it would have to occur off it instead. I decided that I was going to set up a new agreement with one of the restaurants that we didn't send guests to. That fact alone should have triggered an alarm bell in my head, but it barely registered as I bowled into the restaurant one morning and told them that I was thinking of sending our guests to them for dinner on Wednesday nights, if we could agree the right price.

Woodsy didn't stop me as I duly did the deal and sold it to a group of unwitting guests. On the night in question, I couldn't wait to hear all about the phenomenal Tarentaise food that they were no doubt devouring, so I went down to the restaurant and ventured inside.

What greeted me was like a scene from Fawlty Towers. Half of the menu wasn't available, and the service was terrible. One of the guest's chair legs had given way underneath him when he sat down. As I was being told about this, I was ushered to the other side of the table to inspect a side salad, which contained a small furry caterpillar. Lesson learned – it was the first and last week of my little commercial venture.

My penchant for checking in on the local bars in Val Claret, became well known, and had you needed a rep on a Wednesday, whilst you would have struggled to find any of the others, who were somewhere on the mountain, there was a good chance you'd find me in *Fish Tank*, chatting to the owner, Jeremy, about whatever I had just read in that day's UK paper.

Occasionally I would call in at *Couloir*, run by Chris (or 'Baldy' as he was unoriginally, yet universally known). *Couloir* hosted many of our management team's Sunday night dinners, as well as a phenomenal seven course extravaganza on Christmas Day. Their specialty was 'High Altitude Beef' which was cooked in a cream and mustard sauce and finished at the table on a small gas heater.

Dropping in one evening enroute to my apartment, I found Baldy and an acquaintance of his attempting to work their way through a bottle of black sambuca. Never one to shy away from a challenge of this nature, I helpfully offered to assist, and by the time we had finished, we had made a significant dent in a second bottle. Whilst my head took a pounding, my wallet got away scot-free. Without doubt, the bar that everyone spent the most time in was *Jam Bar*, which was ironic, given its size – it was more like a broom cupboard than a bar. It was strictly a Seasonaire bar, guaranteed to always be devoid of guests. Its name had a double meaning, as well as being tiny, 'Jam' was a reference to the two brothers who owned it, Jamie and Morgan.

# 10

# Vendredi

Before you knew it, the week had passed by in a blur, and it was Friday, a day accompanied by the dreaded realisation that another transfer day was just around the corner. Our quiz night provided the final evening's entertainment and was proceeded by the weekly full company staff meeting, held at a resort hotel, and chaired by Woodsy.

This was a chance for the entire staff to regroup. Customer Survey Questionnaires (or CSQ's) were always a hot topic. These had to be completed by the guests on departure, and in sufficient quantity and standard throughout the season for us to be eligible to receive our end of season bonus. Most meetings involved an animated Woodsy trying to ascertain why one (or both) of these criteria had not been met the previous week.

The chalet staff would then receive their guestlists for the forthcoming week, (including the dreaded list of dietary requirements), the logistics of the laundry changes for each chalet would be confirmed and the reps would receive their collection lists for the outgoing and incoming guests. With that, the meeting would draw to a close, signalling the end of one week and the start of the next.

# 11

# Un bréf repit

I'm probably not alone in saying there were times as the season wore on, when the repetition of the week and the claustrophobic nature of living in a ski resort got on top of me. In these moments, I always took a moment to look around. I would generally be under a cloudless blue sky, superimposed by the crisp, clean lines of the brilliant white mountains. Most of the people you saw were on holiday, laughing, skiing, drinking. Music would be pumping out of the bars.

I'd contrast this with what I imagined I would be doing in Putney; escaping the cold, wet, grey weather by scuttling down into the underground, where I would be squeezed into a carriage with my head stuck in someone's armpit, just so that I could pay the rent at the end of the month. I always came to the same conclusion – I was lucky to be where I was, doing what I was doing.

It was normal for people to start feeling a touch of the 'season blues', which was why, at the midpoint of the season, Skiworld arranged for all the staff to have an away day at Lake Annecy, near Albertville. It was only a couple of hours from resort, but it felt like another world. There was no snow, no chalets, and no guests.

This would be the only time in six months that the entire staff would descend beyond Bourg St Maurice. On arrival we didn't make the most of the scenery, but headed instead straight to a local bar, where we proceeded to stay for the rest of the day, drinking Guinness (another novelty) in the sunshine.

The coach trip back was riotous, with some wearing very little on account of their dips in the lake (some voluntary, others less so). At some point in the proceedings, I was relieved of my pants as they were the victim of a forceful 'wedgie', administered by a certain Northern Irish colleague. The drinking carried on back at resort into the wee small hours, providing a much-needed reset for all concerned.

# 12

# Printemps

The season was divided into sections by the 'big' weeks – Christmas, February half term, and Easter, when guests were paying top dollar, and the pressure was really on to deliver. After Easter, the sun shone, new snow rarely made an appearance, and the prices fell accordingly. After such an intense period, the warmer weather, combined with the lower expectations of the guests, ushered in an end of term feel, and we spent many enjoyable late afternoons drinking *pichets* of Rosé following a day skiing in not much more than salopettes, hoodies, and our personalised bobble hats.

The hats were created by a fellow Seasonaire, Lou, who worked for a different tour operator, but who was a regular in *Jam Bar*. To supplement her income, she put her considerable talent for knitting to good use, by making hats for fellow resort workers. The five of us duly ordered ours, with our own colour schemes, and our respective nicknames emblazoned on the front. Mine was red, with a black pompom, and 'Bambi' in big black lettering across the front.

Our Seasonaire hoodies were sky blue, with white lettering, and whilst every high school up and down the country has now adopted the tradition for its leavers, at the time, they were still very much associated with ski seasons, rather than school kids.

On the back were the names (and nicknames) of every member of the resort staff, whilst both arms were bedecked with logos of our 'unofficial partners', which included ski brands, Tignes bars, and even the boxed wine that we served the guests every night! We skied in them, drank in them, and laughed in them. It was a badge of honour, and whilst I haven't worn mine in years, it remains a treasured possession.

In March, I celebrated my 26th Birthday. The chalet staff had a love of fancy dress parties, and I decided to try and harness this by creating my own themed birthday party. Given my place of work prior to the season, and my wholly inappropriate choice of footwear during the training week, a 'Sloane Ranger' themed party seemed a good choice.

I wanted to have the party at a venue off the beaten track, and as luck would have it, had recently discovered a bar in Le Lac called *Café Rouge*, which was frequented mainly by the French locals rather than tourists, and was big enough to host a potentially large group.

Despite inviting all and sundry, I knew it would only take another gathering on the same night to render my party just another little management team soirée, but as it turned out, I needn't have worried. The turnout was humbling, as was the effort that everyone had gone to with the dress theme. The girls in particular, had gone to extraordinary lengths, perhaps seeing this as an opportunity to air their smarter outfits, which had probably been packed more in hope than expectation.

The locals looked on incredulously as the bar slowly filled with bouffant hair styles, topped with designer sunglasses. Necks were surrounded by multiple strands of pearls, whilst wrists jangled with bracelets and bangles. Cashmere scarves were everywhere.

Additional creative flourishes included a homemade pony club rosette, and a silver spoon, which was clutched by its owner for the entire night. I, like most of the other men, went with the Sloane standard issue – formal shirt (with the collar 'popped' for added emphasis), tucked into chinos, the bottoms of which met loafer clad feet.

It was a brilliant and memorable night, due in no small part to the large turnout. The part of me still suffering from imposter syndrome felt a sense of acceptance, that perhaps this was confirmation from my peers of my Seasonaire status. Then again, maybe they just had nothing better to do that night - I suppose I'll never know!

# 13

# Derniers jours

The shutdown of the season was phased, with chalets being closed and deep cleaned, ready to be handed back to their owners for the summer months, when Tignes would be transformed from a winter wonderland to an alpine adventure land for scores of swimmers, cyclists and walkers.

Fortunately, none of my chalets were owned by the exacting individual who insisted on checking off every knife, fork, plate, glass and mug from the property's original inventory, and who apparently became more and more perplexed each year as to why so few of the original articles in question remained, (and why those that did, appeared more used than they had been the previous year.)

Staff whose properties were closing were given their leaving dates, when they would board the bus for the long journey home. There were three staff departure dates, and I was to be in the final one. Woodsy, me, Will, Cat and a skeleton staff would operate the last weeks of the season with a handful of properties. Although I was ready to go home, I took a perverse enjoyment in the knowledge that I would be there until the bitter end. Knowing that this was an experience I was unlikely to ever repeat, I wanted to squeeze every last drop out of it.

The shutdown procedure was the same in Val D'Isère, and our final boozy midweek trip across the valley coincided with the closure of Skiworld's hotel there, *the Cortina*. It's fair to say that there was a difference in opinion between the office staff in Bourg who stated that the remaining alcohol in the bar would be used during the following season, and the hotel staff, who decided they couldn't risk it going to waste. We dutifully decided to help them in their quest.

As the sun started to slowly announce a new day, Matt, with his spiritual side now well lubricated, decided that we should march to the top of a hill and watch the sun rise on what would be our final morning together as a group.

After much climbing, not helped by our unsuitable dress and drunken demeanour, we reached the summit, only to find that due to the low cloud the sunrise wasn't visible. It was at this point that the Tignes contingent realised that we had to get back to resort to run the final staff 'Valley Rally' of the season.

The Valley Rally was a mountain point to point course that the reps devised for the chalet staff. On arrival at each check point (manned by us) there would be a challenge, typically involving an unpleasant alcoholic drink like *genepy*. A vile local brew, it was green in colour, and the most acquired of acquired tastes.

This was the first time in my life that I had pulled a genuine 'all nighter' – Lord knows who drove us back as he or she would have been in the same state, but I arrived back at my apartment safe and sound at about 8am, an hour before I was required back on the mountain.

My apartment didn't have a standalone shower, just an attachment connected to the bath taps. I had therefore become accustomed to having baths rather than showers, but in my current state, I had never been more in need of a revitalising power shower. Instead, the warm bath water proved to be an effective alternative to the bed which I desperately craved, and rather predictably, I dozed off.

Waking with a start, I hurriedly got my ski gear on, grabbed my skis and in an even more shambolic and chaotic state than normal, made my way to the slopes. At least I didn't perform my usual trick of meeting the guests that we were to guide for the day in *Le Lac*, before realising that my lift pass was still in my apartment in *Val Claret*.

The atmosphere was very different in those final weeks in so much as the entire resort staff (such as it was) now socialised together each night. One memorable evening started with another highly enjoyable dinner in *Couloir* as 'Baldy' bid us farewell in fine style, and ended several hours later, with everyone's faces covered in black soot, a result of numerous games of the 'Ibble Dibble' drinking game.

I vividly remember the final transfer day of the season – with only a handful of guests, and no one coming in to resort to replace them, it was a straightforward affair, and the bus picked the guests up directly from the chalet. As it pulled away, I ran after it and feigned a playful kick in its direction, with a feeling of relief, and a sense of satisfaction at a job (occasionally) well done.

Because there were so few of us still to leave resort, our departure was strangely subdued. We had taken a full company photo on the occasion of the first set of departures, and now the last few stragglers were climbing aboard and settling down for the twelve-hour journey that lay ahead.

More goodbyes took place when we reached Victoria coach station, and eventually the group that had subsequently boarded the tube had been whittled down to just me and 'Bee Gee'. We were now all that remained of each other's seasons, a thought not lost on the big fella as my station approached and I was given a big (and slightly tearful) bear hug. He, and my one and only ski season then disappeared into the darkness of the tunnel.

And just like that, it was all over.

# 14

# Fins et débuts

I knew I would never do another season, and even if I had, I doubt it could ever have topped that experience. Many others who either had done seasons previously or went on to do more maintain that Tignes '06 – '07 is at the top of the pile, and this despite us experiencing well below average levels of snow that season.

It was a clearly defined six-month period in my life – everything and everyone involved bookended in a single time and place. Nothing characterised this better than the nickname that fate (and Matt) bestowed on me in Courchevel. The result was that my name, the most basic and fundamental identifier of oneself, was suddenly, and comprehensively replaced for six months by an alter ego.

No longer Tom, a Twenty something trying to climb the greasy pole in London, I was Bambi, a rookie Seasonaire who was learning on the job. I know of more than one person who admitted that by the season's end, they still didn't know my real name! Many still don't, for Bambi lives on to this day amongst the group of people who shared that little part of the French Alps with me all those years ago.

My ski season also brought an end to my Three-and-a-half-year stint in London. I moved back to Yorkshire for the Summer, intending to return to London in the Autumn to job and flat hunt. However, fate decreed that this plan never materialised, as I settled back in Harrogate, eventually meeting the girl who would become my wife and mother to our three children, so perhaps I owe Skiworld a far greater debt of gratitude than it would at first appear.

# 15

# Réflexions d'un Seasonaire

Without doubt, the most challenging part of my time as a resort rep was managing the staff. Of the four pairs of chalet staff that I started the season with, only one pair remained by its end. Changes were occasionally forced on us through season ending skiing injuries, but more commonly they were for disciplinary reasons. Some simply couldn't stay the course. Of my original staff of eight, I must have been through twice that amount by the season's end.

I had staff who served pesto to a guest with a nut allergy (luckily without serious consequences). I had a staff member who threatened his fellow host with a kitchen knife. I had staff who failed to turn up to cook breakfast for their guests because they got too drunk the night before. I had chalet staff cooking three course dinners for their guests for whom a pot noodle would have been considered a culinary victory.

At one point during the season, *Chalet Francois*, was being run by a pair of likely lads who, whilst well meaning, were too easily distracted by the lure of the mountain by day, and the bars by night. Having failed to produce a cake for afternoon tea (a daily mandatory in all Skiworld properties), I was quietly taken aside by one of the guests, who proceeded to read me the list of offences that my staff had been charged with. The missing cake had clearly been the final straw after a few days of poor cooking, served in an untidy chalet.

Finding the accused sitting together in a bar, I explained that the guests were giving them one final chance, which was more than fair. They responded the right way, and when I went into the chalet the following afternoon to see how afternoon tea was being received, I was greeted by a huge spread, complete with gingham tablecloth and a cake that the WI would have been proud of. I was somewhat surprised therefore when the same guest motioned to me. Any thoughts I harboured of being congratulated on my managerial ability were quickly extinguished when I saw what they were holding in their hand. A jar of jam, with a thick, furry layer of mould on the top of it.

It wasn't all bad though. I also had staff for whom nothing was too much effort, and who always went the extra mile, taking real pride in the cleanliness of their properties and the quality of the food that they produced. I was often a beneficiary, as there were often spare portions, resulting in me surreptitiously eating a different course in each chalet's kitchen as I made my evening rounds.

Guests could be equally unpredictable and varied - from debauched students like the ones I encountered at the beginning of the season, to young professionals, and well to do retired groups who were well accustomed to their chalet host's slight indiscretions. Sometimes the chalet was a single group, other times it was made up of multiple groups which made for a very different, slightly fractured atmosphere.

I had guests who literally crawled to dinner after well and truly overindulging in the après ski. I had guests who were difficult, rude, and impatient. Equally, I had guests who were generous, kind, and understanding, often when they had no right to be. On one miraculous and sadly fleeting occasion, a guest became slightly more than a guest, which at least allowed me to sample one of my chalet host's breakfasts!

One evening, I had been doing my evening rounds of the chalets, and was about to leave, when the host of one of the properties asked me very calmly and politely if he could have a word with me downstairs in the basement. Unlike many of the staff who were young and looked like they would blow over in a stiff breeze, he was a big man, easily the oldest member of staff, and a very talented cook and host. He'd worked around the world, but this was his first experience of a ski season.

He and his girlfriend ran the chalet immaculately, returning consistently strong customer survey scores week in, week out. Whilst they didn't present me with any of the challenges that some of my younger, less experienced staff did, it's fair to say that their expectation levels were far higher as a result.

When they had first arrived in resort, they complained about the room that had been allocated to them and I had managed to find them alternative accommodation arrangements, but despite my best efforts, it was a frustration which was always simmering under the surface. Now, a few months into the season, that frustration boiled over.

My confusion as to why this conversation needed to take place in the basement rather than in the chalet above soon became apparent as the ambush was launched. What followed was a one-way screaming match that lasted for about fifteen minutes. Like a Sergeant Major addressing a Private, his nose was almost touching mine as he let rip, flecks of spit occasionally crashing into my face.

On more than one occasion I felt certain that he was going to hit me. I left feeling shocked, upset, angry, and seriously wondering what I was still doing in resort. At that moment I couldn't see how I could possibly make it to the end of the season. Going back to my apartment and stewing would have only deepened my gloom.

Fortunately, Cathers and Foz had offered to cook dinner for us that night in their apartment. John and Will's flat was over the corridor from theirs, and as I walked in, having got the bus down to Le Lac, the four of them were chatting away in candlelight, music playing, wine glasses in hand. There was soon one in my hand too, and it wasn't long before I was cathartically relaying the events of the evening to them.

Before long, what had seemed like an insurmountable issue had been reduced, through a combination of red wine and camaraderie to just another occupational hazard. It was siege mentality, and it was vital to my ability to navigate a few dark moments of self-doubt.

Resilience was certainly an important characteristic when it came to dealing with the build quality of the properties that I managed. I received a portent of things to come on my very first visit to *Tichot* which had been newly refurbished. As I went to open a door, the handle snapped clean off in my hand. Fortunately, this proved to be a singular occurrence, which was more than could be said for the other three properties I was responsible for.

*Valerie, Dominique,* and *Francois* had a communal spa in the basement, consisting of a sauna, steam room and jacuzzi, for which the guests paid a premium. Every week, the thermostat in the sauna would trip out, and after a couple of day's use, the water in the jacuzzi went from being crystal clear, to something resembling a swamp. By the time it had been drained, refilled and reheated, the week was almost over.

Domestic building regs, combined with facilities that were hopelessly inadequate for the number of people using them, were not excuses angry guests wanted to hear – all I could do was apologise, week in, week out. Their grievances would usually be aired in their CSQ scores, with my perceived role in the saga ranging from co-conspirator to innocent bystander, depending on the opinion of the author.

The score allocated to the rep by the guests each week often depended on how many incidents had occurred, and how many of them (in their opinion at least) were within our power to resolve. You could receive good, bad, or indifferent scores, sometimes fair, often less so, but it was something that I became more accepting of as the season wore on.

Frustrations, whether caused by guests, staff, or buildings, could all be exorcised in the intimate surroundings of *Jam Bar*. On setting foot in 'Jam', you were always amongst friends – it was rather like a Sixth Form common room where you could let your guard down and blow off some steam at any time of the day or night. It was so small that unused beer barrels were often stored inside along the wall. After any kind of company social, we'd always end the night there, and I would generally be volunteered by my peers to make any required announcements. The barrels proved to be useful pulpits from which to preach, and I became adept at balancing with a foot on each side of the rim, waxing lyrical with pint in hand, as a scrum of bodies jostled for space below me.

As I write these words, I can scarcely believe that Eighteen years have passed since our little team met each other for the first time. Now scattered across the country, we have become husbands or wives, mothers or fathers. Despite rarely seeing each other in the time that has passed, when we banter on Whatsapp, the memories of the times and places we hold dear, and that are unique to us, come flooding back.

I feel so incredibly lucky to have been part of the Tignes 2006/7 Skiworld team, and to have met the people that I did. Like a band of brothers, we will forever be bonded by the people and events that only we and a few others experienced, 2,100 meters up in the French Alps.

30

# 16

# Mon équipe

There are memories of the individual members of the group which still make me smile all these years later. For reasons of impartiality, they appear in alphabetical order!

### Catherine (Cathers)
As mentioned earlier, Cathers was the mother hen of the group, extolling the virtues of doing things properly. A 'roll your sleeves up and get on with it' attitude was tempered by a much softer, caring side. She would often cook dinner for the five of us and sitting round the table together in her and Foz's little apartment really felt like a home from home.

Whilst hardly contributing to the sartorial elegance of the resort myself (my orange salopettes were quickly nicknamed the 'Chewit pants'), Cathers would often appear at Friday staff meetings dressed in some extraordinary ensembles, consisting of green bobble hat, blue hoodie, orange board shorts and Ugg boots, which led me on one occasion to enquire (in a rather loud voice), who (or what) she had come dressed as.

My abiding memory of Cathers will always be when she came to my rescue on that infamous first day on the mountain. Plenty could have stopped. Only one person did. It's no coincidence that it was Cathers.

### Jess (Foz)

If you asked Jess her opinion on something, you knew that you would always get a straight answer, even if that answer was along the lines of *'just tell them to f\*ck off'*, followed by the trademark cackle. Talking to Foz about a problem always made it better – even if it was just to have a good laugh about it.

One day, we saw a poster on a lamp post near *Jam Bar*. It had a picture of a dog on it, a contact number, and the word *'Perdu'* (lost). We acknowledged it as we passed, then thought no more about it. It was only a couple of days later, when seeing the same poster and assuming the dog was still lost, that Jess exclaimed *'oh no they haven't found it yet – poor little Perdu'*. Her lack of French vocab had us in stitches for days.

## John (John Boy)

John didn't suffer fools gladly be they staff or guests. His work ethic was second to none (his twin brother may argue second to himself...!) and he would always go the extra mile for anyone, as long as he felt that those efforts were necessary, and that they would be appreciated. Where he and his brother differed, was around the subject of conflict resolution, which was hilariously demonstrated one night in Val D'Isère.

We were on one of our Tuesday nights out when John realised that he couldn't find his jacket. Slowly, the horrifying truth, namely that his not inexpensive coat had been stolen from under his nose dawned on him. The horror quickly changed to a simmering rage, as he began to describe what he would do to the perpetrator of the crime, should he ever come across him.

As it turned out, he didn't have long to wait for his opportunity. On leaving the bar, John saw a man wearing a jacket which looked remarkably similar to his own. He approached the man to take a closer look, and having done so, realised that it was in fact *his* jacket. Matt, sensing the impending fireworks had followed in his slipstream, and chose this moment to put himself between the two men as the accusations began to fly.

While John circled, eyeing his prey like a lion in a gladiatorial arena, Matt spoke to the hapless thief, asking him what his mother would think of him for committing such a shameful act. Shame in one's own actions Matt felt, would strike a heavier blow than even John could muster (although he'd doubtless have had a go). In the end, the protagonists dispersed peacefully, the burning shame felt by the would-be thief, complimented by the cosy heat being provided by John's jacket, which had been reacquainted with its rightful owner.

## Will (Winks)

I probably spent more time with Will than anyone else in the group. I ski guided with him (or rather he guided while I tried to keep up.) On the rare occasions that I chose to venture on to the mountain for a recreational ski, it was often with Will, ('*Bambi and Winks have gone for a love ski*' was how the others used to describe it.) Off the mountain we might go for a 'Lilly burger' together, Lilly being the name of a rather pretty waitress who worked in one of the resort snack bars, and for whom Will had taken quite a shine.

The reason we were happy in each other's company (and that perhaps the others were glad of it) was a bizarre personality trait that we both had; namely, an ability to quote entire sections from films – and not just any films, but the same ones. It was as though we had shared a sofa for years.

Unsurprisingly, the others made themselves scarce when the *Withnail and I,* or *Top Gun* quotes (which were fired at each other like a game of linguistic tennis) started, confident in the knowledge that the match could go on for some time. Although we now reside at opposite end of the country, these linguistic duels have continued to take place via text message in the ensuing years.

## Chris (Woodsy)

It would have been remiss of me not to mention Woodsy, for it was under his command that the five of us were able to operate so well. Whilst almost always laid back and easy going, there were times when he would leave you in no doubt about what he wanted – the sparing use of this more dictatorial style merely confirmation of the seriousness of the situation, and his eagerness to see it resolved.

Woodsy banned me from entering his flat in my boots which has taken on a fairly pungent odour on account of them rarely being completely dry – and once even ordered me to wash my feet in his bath! His two stock expressions were *'bumbling'* and *'sub average banter'* – both of which he would use frequently to describe either a lack of organisational efficiency, or a lack of wit. Unsurprisingly, we were often on the receiving end of both observations!

Now a commercial airline pilot, I can only hope that he doesn't ever utter one of his other stock expressions while the flight deck microphone is switched on as it may result in numerous customer complaints. Many was the time that we would hear Woodsy utter it to describe some unfortunate whose actions, consciously or otherwise, had fallen foul of his standards. Its utterance would be followed immediately by the familiar laugh – *'What a c\*\*\*!'*